BLOOD RISES

ESSENTIAL POETS SERIES 278

Guernica Editions Inc. acknowledges the support
of the Canada Council for the Arts and the Ontario Arts Council.
The Ontario Arts Council is an agency of the Government of Ontario.
We acknowledge the financial support of the Government of Canada.

David Haskins

BLOOD RISES

GUERNICA
EDITIONS

TORONTO • CHICAGO • BUFFALO • LANCASTER (U.K.)
2020

Michael Mirolla, editor
Cover and Interior Design: Rafael Chimicatti
Cover Image: *The Phantom Hunter*, William Blair Bruce
Guernica Editions Inc.
287 Templemead Drive, Hamilton (ON), Canada L8W 2W4
2250 Military Road, Tonawanda, N.Y. 14150-6000 U.S.A.
www.guernicaeditions.com

Distributors:
Independent Publishers Group (IPG)
600 North Pulaski Road, Chicago IL 60624
University of Toronto Press Distribution (UTP),
5201 Dufferin Street, Toronto (ON), Canada M3H 5T8
Gazelle Book Services, White Cross Mills
High Town, Lancaster LA1 4XS U.K.

First edition.
Printed in Canada.

Legal Deposit – Third Quarter
Library of Congress Catalog Card Number: 2019949201
Library and Archives Canada Cataloguing in Publication
Title: Blood rises / David Haskins.
Names: Haskins, David, 1944- author.
Description: Poems.
Identifiers: Canadiana 20190174048 | ISBN 9781771835381 (softcover)
Classification: LCC PS8565.A725 B56 2020 | DDC C811/.54—dc23

To Shirl, my beloved for 31 of her 52 years,
and for all that remain of mine.

Were we to enter
death alone
that bird with flaming breast
would welcome us
into its scarlet embrace

—JAMES DEAHL, "Eau de lune"
in *Travelling the Lost Highway*

Contents

Part 1

where the needle stops

Waiting

for Wayne Johnston

Here in the darkness is where the ice begins
and the air crystallizes in your throat.
Here is where the light takes
months to arrive and depart.

A scrap of paper with your name
lies buried somewhere near a flag
as pointless and necessary as space.
Here is where you sang hallelujahs.

Here is where the needle stops
where any step you take is south
and going back is going on.
You stand alone with what you've won

snow blind, frost bit, toeless, frozen.
The final victory on top of the world
buckles your knees, a prayerful effigy
still waiting for the light.

On Voting Liberal

It's all about balance
not slipping off the rails
how the earth keeps safe distance
from sun and moon

the tension that holds the space
between you and another
between the face you prepare
and the one you suspect
is running your trains on time

are you so surprised that a tropical sea
covered these northern climes
or that mastodon and mammoth bones
hide among your vegetables?

where does a train wander
when its rails meet in the perspective?

the proven orbit does not
protect you from impact
and balance merely postpones
going nova
and then the black hole
of being and nothingness

if the centre cannot forever hold
and you expend your one chance
on false testimony, lose yourself
in mediocrity, would you not wish
to have cracked open restraint
enough to see even once
the dark side of the moon?

I Do Remember Untersberg

1

Climbing inside a descending cloud
my feet chance upon a young girl's face
a plaque beside the forgotten place
where she slipped on loose gravel
tumbled to her death so far below
they could neither retrieve her broken corpse
nor protect it from the kites and hawks

Had she too been lost in a cloud
that day she aspired to a new view
over the top, a mountaineer's dream
when her boot dislodged the stones
that bounced and gathered speed
beside her, each a hidden marker
on the bread crumb trail to her death

As though the mountain welcomed her
and would not send her back
into the world of lesser men
I am on my knees inches from her face
The icy fog entombs me like one of Franklin's men
whose horrid grimace answered that pointless forage

2

On a summer slope ripe with saxifrage
orchid, rock jasmine, edelweiss
the trail rough cut through turf and shale
the hot July sun scorching the safe ascent
in my coltish nerve, I leaped across
the tedious switchback curves, straight for the top
stumbling through hollows and outcrops
across meadow mined with treachery

I heard the scrape of boot on stone
and knew not what I had begun
The missile sprung unbounded
in an arc falling from my sight
bouncing down upon a pasture, or a traveller
walking in the sweet morning's warmth

I waited for blessed silence
and took the certain path home
hoping not to be seen, not to find
A mountain absorbs a man's murderous folly
as though nothing may change
except the man

Forgiven

The day my sister died a butterfly
                    leaped and hovered
climbed the glass, landed
                    on my jean jacket shoulder
(the butterfly, the first of the year;
                    my sister, the last of my family).
I walked my visitor to the car
                    and stopped, and waited.

Sheltered from the huzzah of wind
                    it opened its wings, breathing light
flared its red ribbon against my denim.
                    I sensed its raspy feet
as though reluctant to leave
                    it wanted to carry me too
as she did when we were children
                    in the same morning bed
and our dog had been killed on the highway
                    and gone to heaven
and was watching us make up stories
                    and cry in each other's arms.

I didn't notice the moment it let go
                    bobbing and weaving up over the roof
as though it had never touched me
                    once a boy chasing butterflies
through weed fields to pin and set
                    in their chloroformed death mask.
Back then I learned you must kill beauty to keep it.
                    This day we parted ways.

April 18, 2012

Flight of Geese

Air flows on gypsy violins
       through the morning glade
Mile high honkers ride the billows
       hanging from sound waves
I search the trees' tall surround
       Turning, I face rain
Cold fear washes from my skin
       and slow deliberate pain

As the first V enters the circle
I feel my centre rise above stone

       "Did you see them?"
       Turning, in the grey wind
       I face your naked body
       certain as alabaster
       and as the dove, holy

Eyes that behold beauty
fall to earth, wounded

Roberts Creek, BC

Punting on the Cherwell

for Marianne in Oxford

A practised athlete
sure footed, javelin poised
you looked ahead, charted a true line
for our rudderless raft;
I lay in the bottom and tracked
where we had travelled
in our Janus craft
casting in memory these
few springtime moments.

With certain grace
you walked your hands down the pole
lifting it from the glassy whorl
slid it between the water's folds
and drove it down to the river bed
levering your weight to lift us forward
the next measure in our silent passage

past college peaks beyond the yellow rape
past the sprawling chestnut limb
where lazed a grinning Cheshire cat
and on beneath old Magdalen bridge
where supplicant whispering rushes
brushed against the barge bottom.

Every paradise is home to someone;
skittering skating water boatmen

mud puppies and moorhens
flashing trout and kingfishers
mad queens and playing cards.

Sudden stretching branches trapped you
in a filigree of teardrop streamers
bent you low in a surfer's crouch –
any jolt or shift could topple you
send us both into the murky panic.

At a bend where the current carved the bank
mother swan nested on her broad mat of sticks
plaited two feet above the water's height.
To get a closer look, we entered
the arc of father's domain, and slipped
between him and his life-mate.
He fanned out his wing feathers
stretched tall his slender neck
glared down a solemn warning
and jerked his head as if to strike.
Guardian and nurturer, punter and passenger
mismatched dyads caught in a skirmish …

You pushed us on to safer shores
an Eden hung with purple bellflowers
of a hundred-year-old Paulownia tree.
That night, outsiders, arm in arm
we walked the empty cobbled street
beneath the Bridge of Sighs, and soon
we came upon St Mary's tower
and wondered 'neath a starless sky
whether the moon would hit the spire.

Morning Coffee at Station One

There's never much room for the truth
while those who believe they know
all the answers suppress the questions
—Chris Pannell, "We went out naked"

Two young women talk at a table
An infant wanders away from his mother
sucks the flip lid on a plastic squeeze bottle
The coffee house is a reclaimed fire station
the pacifier a repurposed lotion tube
Nothing may be taken at face value

The toddler watches me choose my chair
careful not to spill my cup
His eyes are wide, his perfect face upturned
curious to mind what else is there
besides his mother his stroller and her purse
I cannot but smile   He notices

takes his only toy from his lips
reaches out and offers it to me
asking me to join with him
share his tabula rasa wonder
a one-year-old and a seventy-one-year-old
momentary travellers at the edge of the new world

His mother sees our subtle bond
and rises to retrieve her young –
he has stepped where he should not
where she did not lead him –

and who am I to take from her
the right to introduce him to a world
that will confound him in his time

Not knowing what waits beyond the moment
he bounces on her knee and frets

Part 2

the wild among us

War Canoe

we set out upon the northern sea
as though it were a backwater
our blades tearing at the swells
like spawning salmon
our hearts full of war

alongside the gunwale
the great shadow exploded
up and over our heads
a weightless leviathan
its eye cast down upon us
and lunged back into the sea
and sounded

the wake of its flukes
did not swamp us
nor deter us
from our course
though our drum skin
did not tremble
and we paddled
quiet as the deeps

Urban Fox

In the filtered light from a street lamp
at the end of a cobbled alley
she hunches down to watch me
and seeing I mean her no harm
slinks to the farthest corner
her stealth drenched in shadow.

Long ago the city fortress
called us from the starved fields.
Now it brings the wild among us,
miles from pasture, copse, and brook,
this ragged waif plagued with mange,
an opportunist fallen from grace.

A disenfranchised citizen-savage
scavenger of human refuse,
she prowls the markets of south London
to feed her mewling kits, their den
warmed with hair she pulled from her skin.

She shows no pride in owning the night –
like a beleaguered spy come in from the cold
or some old drunk nestled under cardboard –
depending on no one's kindness,
as fearless as the rats she beds down with
and, if she has to, eats.

I want her to be the fox the prince's
horse and hound and redcoat riders
chase around my Tiffany shade
never run to ground or torn apart
when blood rises in the teeth of dogs.

Or the glass-eyed fox my late aunt draped
about her neck at Sunday service
the perfect tail curved down one shoulder
head and front paws down the other
watching me reach up to touch
the soft seductive fur without
interrupting her solemn prayers.

I don't belong in this survivor's street;
for now she knows she has the upper hand.
One day she'll chew her black boot off
to free her from a leg hold trap
and all her cunning will bleed out slow
the wild waning in her slit eyes
the mysterious sisterhood of fox.

Sand Digger

On the shovel, thin slices of sand
scraped from rock ice, loose and light
deceptive in the shirt sleeve February morning.
Water seeps into boot prints
sweat wets the small of the back
new muscles ache under shoulder blades
heave the filled pail onto the first step.

Eyes lift to a cyan sky
cloudless, clean as the born season,
lift to a line of flapping wings
glaring white in slow repeats
lift to thin necks stretching east
to the island gathering in Quebec
where these 36 will rest with 80
thousand snow geese coming home.

Fingers curl under the rim
lungs fill and lock
the back strains, the body lurches
a foot searches the next step.
Eyes measure the cliff's height
to the waiting barrow and sieve.
The mind considers the overhead corridor
where white birds passed without complaint.

November

Gulls wheel low in the indiscriminate white
above my garden, their flight paths chaotic, frantic
barely missing each other. The sky is still, close.
The birds sense it's not yesterday's shiny pleasure
but a harbinger of cold times, storm season
gales stripping colours off tangled black branches.

They've come inland off the lake to check us out
curious to know how we survive, shut in our boxes
without going crazy. For them, every day is a risk.
Last year some were trapped in the grasp of lake ice
the cold boring through their sheen until they froze
hunched lumps white on white too stuck to fall over.

A few dip down into my garden. No fish for them
inside these fences, no pond in the covered pool.
They wheel back to the heights, off to the delta
where the Forty creek enters the lake, to wait –
they do what they can, then take what comes
the provident drizzle, the empty sky.

Winter

Interracial trees
bare themselves
tired from jostling
for position
in the race
for light

For one night
my tree
harbours your stars
then
is buried alive
in white

Loon

on the radio, 'TV on the Radio'
a boy burns ants with a magnifying glass
a landing loon brakes on a Muskoka lake
a lone pine fills with stupefied doves
a red canoe tilts on a drifting log
a one-legged heron stands among reeds
drowned deadheads and softball lilies

heat flutes the air over the lake
a turtle bakes on a log island garden
a novel is set down beside cold coffee
someone's heart beats through slow sleep

a speedboat, racing into rumour
rears up and back flips
a body slams into concrete water
the loon heads under
the explosion switched off
ripples slap shore rock
crescendo diminuendo

acorns drop without warning
like August stars
giggling girls fall from a diving board
a Blackberry vibrates off the picnic table
the loon pops up
half a mile away

A Hard Life

expect a stone to sink

some stones float in defiance
their perforations stuffed with air

some stones quake under their weight
when the ground shifts beneath their feet

some stones roll over each other
passionate tumblers tossed in the current

some stones rise up burst and flame
like dandelions through concrete

some stones lean in all confidential-like
listening to the tales of old

some stones stand still as mountains
gleam against the wind's caress

some stones careen through space
by chance find us looking up

expect a stone to fall

Spring Rain

A chunk of land with our neighbour's silver birch
slides into the lake like a calving glacier.
Talk on the tube says the system has stalled
rains rise up on the unyielding earth
the escarpment a raw lip for new-channelled falls
and we down below in the flood plain fear
for the night's invisible deluge to fall.

A man in olive uniform said Duck and Cover
cower under desks or line hallway lockers
when the doomsday clock ticked off minutes
to midnight. Now the race is back on
rockets fly, missiles are tested, bigger bombs
than the levellers of Nagasaki and Hiroshima
as frigate bird politicos puff out their red chests.

This is the new world we've come to expect –
please be advised it's not safe to rebuild here
the climate is changing with every election.
Tomorrow I'll wake to a lake in my garden
sandbags and sump pumps too little too late
brown sludge in my cellar, my house a house-boat.
Nothing is enough. The water keeps rising.

Part 3

cranial teapots, pelvic bowls

Fish Lake

Used to be a lake over there
trout, not big but plentiful
Had a resort on the edge
people came to get away
sit by the water
think about things

One of the guests sold her wedding ring
to help pay for the view
the price of gold is so high

Now they watch trucks
corkscrew up the pit roads
through unnatural haze
of this burst blister

Down east they tunnelled
six miles under ocean
to get their coal
Here they drain Fish Lake
scrape out the gold

There's copper too
just when they stopped making pennies
Maybe we'll get new pipes
won't have to go outside

Down east the companies
dump their tailings into lakes
That's how they kill 'em down there

Will this lake come back?
Not in a baby's baby's lifetime
We have other lakes
they haven't got to yet

Company made us another lake
called it Prosperity Lake
instant nature
stocked it with trout
bigger
fewer

Logging's gone
tree huggers, pine beetles
not much else to do
but the town's still here

Seen the news?
They found gold under Stanley Park

The Fall Kill

I spit on your holy challenge of the hunt
I am sickened by your fresh air, friends and whisky
you red vested mongrel padded with lies
and the hot flush of murder pumping your heart
as you crawl to the edge, sneaking inches
when she lowers her great head to the ears
under water to feed on fat succulents.

What explains your single-minded bloodlust
when you raise the stock, sight the crosshairs
beside her shoulder at the soft place where
the fireball will sear through the nap, and bring
this placid giant crashing to her knees
in a parody of prayer beseeching you
to whom dominion over death is guaranteed
as you hack through her warm neck, your boot
treading her eye like a log, and the splinters
of bone and blood fly from your blade?
The severed head borne aloft on a shield of pine
all so your children will know who's boss.

When I was twelve I spied from some great distance
a yellow-bellied sapsucker drilling a maple tree
and with a lucky shot I blew it off the bark.
My friend smashed its twitching head upon a rock.
I wish you no such mercy.

Are There No Fish in Guatemala?

I haven't mentioned the head for two days.

Today in the mailbox, a manuscript.
Sharing his childhood with his grandchildren
a retired salesman writes about his grandfather
a pulpit-pounding fundamentalist
now a memory in his fin-sharp brain
like the coho runs up the Queen Charlottes' creeks
a 500-pound halibut they hauled alongside the skiff
when he was thirteen, and the salmon
they blew up with gelignite,
gaffed, gutted, and layered in brine.

But I saw it, sandwiched
between a sinking oil rig and the Constitution
between helicopter shots of San Sebastian
and the weeping women
between two blue T-shirted soldiers
with M16s and machetes
who grabbed the wet hair
as though it were the world cup
and they the champions
because they had arrived last.
They had closed its eyes
and muddied it.

He might have been thirteen
and worn an ammo belt.
Perhaps he had wanted this,
the passionate veneration of parts
that fishermen throw away.

As the camera zoomed in
I hoped that the boy had slept through it all
or that he had believed in something.

Are there no fish left to butcher in Guatemala?

Disposition

YouTube slideshow –
a man's naked body is
trussed and hogtied
slashed from shoulders to ankles
exposing sinews
to swarming vultures
that pick his bones clean.
Then his skull is split
and his brains extruded
a final treat
for the obliging birds.

But that is Columbia
there is a drug war.

Video news –
a man squashes a body
into an acid-filled barrel.
He has "disappeared" 300 so far
for a wage of $600 a month.
Out back he grows vegetables
fertilizes them with calcium
from their bones.

But that is Mexico,
thousands are murdered, and this is his job.

CBC movie *Elizabeth* –
men are hanged by short rope
to strangle but not snap the neck,

then revived, drawn and quartered,
their intestines winched up
out of their slit bellies
and held before their screaming eyes
so they can see their own unravelling.

But they were English
probably traitors, a long time ago.

Redacted documents –
Canada delivers a detainee
to foreign hands to be whipped,
starved, frozen, choked, shocked;
our hands being washed of sin.

But they are Afghans
he is a Musl ..., a Talib ...

This is now. We are Canadians. He is a man.

March 28, 2010

A Potter's Ossuary

of fragments
defects
mistakes
failures

cranial teapots
pelvic bowls
rib handles
limb splinters

wedding rings
spectacles
sheaf of hair
hill of shoes

ear necklace
tooth beads
skin lamp
scalp belt

broken trophies
hidden from judgement
stacked sorted
uncounted uncatalogued

nothing to identify
the missing the murdered
nothing to speak
a creator's name

The Reason

I am the cancer wanting more.
I fill my gasoline tank with war.
I drink poverty in coffee and politics in coke.
Children are stitched in the seams of my shirt.
A dirty old man pockets my coin.
Manhattan's canyons are my cocoon.
My daughters are raised by a refugee.
My house is built out of forests that breathe.
Fourteen cameras watch my door.
I am the cancer wanting more.

If not for me they would earn no wage,
grow no flowers, sell no leaves.
That's why there are continents, master and slave;
why religions, righteous apartheid;
why pandemics, generational genocide.
All the four horsemen ride through their homes
but I sleep well in my temperate zone.
I take pride in the stuff I own.
I want to help them turn the page;
if not for me they would earn no wage.

Someone who knows the taste of rats
will have to put them on the boats
and let them in. I am not of their tribe.
I meet them on holiday. I do not bide
at the back of my tent blind from disease
awaiting my killers or my next meal.
I am evolved. Success orphaned me.
Someone will have to do something more
deserving of a parade than winning a war.
Someone who knows the taste of rats.

Part 4

who now can make a nail from earth

Resilience

for Robert Davidson, Haida painter of the transformative
Southeast Wind.

... and hope that the stories that live inside the curl of your
knuckles can be coaxed out one more time
—Richard Wagamese, 2015 Matt Cohen Award Speech

How do you paint the Southeast wind
that blows the pox into every eye
topples totems, turns villages to burial grounds
crashes warriors in a foamy stew
carries off children to an alien language
churns the gravel in the salmon creek beds
cracks the canoe inside the tree?

You pound the red ochre to powder
mix salmon eggs with your spit
doodle a design in thirty seconds
take one whole day to crisp a line
where negative is positive is negative again
the need for yes or no forgotten on the wind
that lifts the killer whale light as air.

Wind moves the line, line leads the eye
eye guides the hand, hand cuts the curve;
charcoal blackens thick skeletal bones
around U-shaped fins, ovoid head,
blowhole, tail, eye already human;
formlines winnow, dissipate energy
away from the numinous beast.

The storm drum rumbles on top of Tow Hill.
The spirit creature breaches from a crack in the past
when the door between worlds was easily opened.
Grab the wind by its kelp hair, pull it into your canoe.
The wind become whale become human tells you
Look back where you came from, then break a new trail
paint the Southeast, and his mother Tomorrow
paint your people's journey through storm and sorrow.

All that remains are moss-covered thresholds
green indentations in the forest floor
a mortuary board, a potlatch pole leaning
ancestral stories ten thousand years old.
A Watchman sits on a log in South Moresby;
the morning fog shrouds the silent sea.
He shares his breakfast with a deer at arm's length
then listens for the breath of the Southeast wind.

A Night at Dildo Run

A power boat thrums across the lake
and then is gone with the sun, the pink
edges of clouds polishing the water gun-metal grey
above the gentle heartbeat of its lapping.

Three campsites down a child calls for his mother.
The mountains swallow his cry. They have heard
all the children come and go;
children of The People who walked across the ice
children of exiles who feared the open sea
children of plunderers who came as gods.
Some left when the sun drove out the seals
some were killed or chased away
some fought each other to own the land.

Dark shapes sleep inches under my feet;
bones, shells, scraps of iron, pilfered
for second use, or fashioned from the red bog
(Who now can make a nail from earth to mend a boat?)
their whispers shimmer like northern lights.

I swat mosquitoes and try to spark a fire
with a barbecue lighter and wet tinder
as they might have done with their fire stones.
Rock, wood, and water
stand silent against the risen moon.
Thousands of miles away you
send an e-mail into the void
asking where I am and whom I am with.
Don't worry, my dear. I am in the company of ghosts.

Dildo Run Provincial Park, Newfoundland

Giantism

Isaac, child of the twenty-first century
crushed into earth under the advance of tractors
razing the forest without heed
for the tiger lily laughing at the thyme.

After the sacrifice of the last generation of fathers
after god flew away on the wings of a raven
not bearing to look upon pine mushrooms
pushing up through the ashes of children
who once searched the sky for the memory of trees
stronger than buttresses, taller than columns
robbed of their places, like Isaac.

The mad descending arctic light
pierces the vaulted canopy of greed
a lightfall tracery of capillaries
across the fallen forest, sucking up
guilt like puffs of poisonous effusion.
The desecration won by fathers on the hillside
has vanquished sons, victors, and the future all.
Deep in the clear-cut's tangled detritus
a ram lies pinned.

Anthropomorphology

Spring's heat gets to him
fucking her in the dirt
five bursts in rapid succession
eight more balanced precariously
on the top branch of a pear tree

his own mile high club
his promise of progeny
and the continuance of his name

then back to work grasping at straws
checking the neighbourhood
for fly-by egg stealers.

His safe-house, a painted schoolhouse
his entrance between the bell and the front door
a hole sized for him, too small for thieves.

He's arranging the furniture, patting it down
so it feels like this year's home
the same web of weeds as last
to the non-sparrow eye.

How like him am I
getting married, building a house
looking out for the young'uns
under the watchful eye of crows.

Pruning Black Raspberries

Last year's canes droop
in a tangle away from the fence
their bark stripped by winter
old fruit clusters left unpicked.

Last summer's yellow-jackets
sucked the purple sugar
sparrows punctured fat seeds
and left the bleeding berries
to rot in the sun that ripened them.

Woody stalks crack limp in the shears;
a few soft stems with split buds
barely hint at new harvest
free to first takers.

Their persistence to reassert themselves
despite disease, destruction, and death
to fulfill their role year after year
with only a little discipline from
someone with a pair of secateurs.

Hard to imagine being without them
a promise broken, a faith betrayed
but wasps and birds will migrate
to apples and pears, and soon
we will revisit these plants
that once covered the naked fence
with branch, leaf and fruit
ever something to anticipate.

A Christmas Morning Poem

Sad and gentle snowflakes swirl
outside my window, lose themselves
in a white sky, reappear
against black branches
wriggle free from the tangle
reluctant to fall on dampening stones.
They beckon me to watch their dance.

More arrive, big floaters following
their curlicue paths to nowhere
seeking companions while there's still time.
Two squirrels chase about the garden.
An undiscovered woodpecker
hammers his way to hidden food.
How does he know? How do any of us know?

Reclamation

He was the first to build a picture window
shear off trees
leaving the tangling roots.
He trimmed the greening earth
and ferreted out weeds
with methodical madness.
The wire-worms slipped deeper down their black holes.

Some white days the lake became sky
and his world stopped at the cliff edge.
The water sucked sand
from under his feet
stole beneath the slope
cracked the surface
and a piece of his world was space.

On limpid winter nights
he slid down the ice banks
while the swells slapped below
like a father admonishing an infant.
What stars,
silent eyes in a midnight forest,
plotted his possibilities?

He moved his chair to the centre of the room
when the wave gathered
like legions on the horizon line
rolling high over the water
a raw emerald curl
swallowing beach and cliff
crashed upon the window

and receded
dropping grey-white mountains on his lawn.
The second ice-blue force
smashed the glass
and spent its last upon his eyes.
Quiescent
he waited for the ice to come.

Part 5
naked again he writes

How to Write a Canadian Poem

Say you are from some bay or cove or tickle
but live in Toronto
Say you read Dylan Thomas
but don't. Read Dylan

Talk of fireflies, blackflies, bones, stones, water, mirrors
Talk of poison ivy and first love in the same breath
Call it a "palimpsest" and acknowledge Earle Birney
Title it "Bushed" and acknowledge every poet before you

Put in something to kill:
a moose in the headlights, a bear, salmon, cod
a car, a culture, the planet, god
Don't kill it till after it stares you down
Don't look for history where there is none
Look for history in trees

Write in chopped
up prose, minus explanation
Call your poems totems, minus punctuation
Make "you" the poet, the reader, a lover
and no one in particular
Claim a hundred words for snow
but call it snow

19/02/82

Snow

Snow slows things down
pushes people out of sight
makes them obedient.
Even the dead must wait
to be trundled to their graves.

Bright ones emerge like newborns
squealing into the shock of cold
to dare the hummocks, slopes and troughs
play out their little survival dramas
in forts and tunnels and tube runs.

This albino aberration
promises the perfection of silence
before fumes and piss and commerce
shrink it to a dirty river of memories
to brag about in ten minutes at Timmy's.

And some scorcher in July
at high noon as the grass burns
a few flakes will fall like hailstones on peaches
an ecstasy of relief, a testament of belief
that the world will turn another revolution.

Feb 16, 2007, at The Dog

en avant, en garde

Tuesday morning, 8 a.m.
Poets at the landfill scrabble
through the effluent of the affluent
clawing for scraps of language
past their best before date.

One hauls away an old butterfly cabinet
and half empty boxes of Alphabits letters
he'll sort out and pin in the drawers
then count the e's, and ponder their e-quality.

Another scores a Venetian blind:
with erasure in mind
she slips out slats to make a staff
for her swan song's notation.

A third scans the electronics bin
for letters of perpetual motion.

A tire-less CCM bike with a rusty tractor seat
drives a barn-full of clanking doodads
into a bluegrass sound soup symphony.

A Slinky lurches down a wordcase
spewing letter-lizards into a blue box.

"End ze tyranny
of
ze
left,"
ze Academy vispos.

Torrents of screeners
in the race for space
send asemic genomes
somewhere over the rainbow.

It's all such fun
this Mad Max poetry
its fuel redacted
and firing pins removed.

p' OM

for Steve McCaffery

in the be begi   was the W   Wor   Wor
the bir birth of   nah nay name
mult multi multipli   (many) l lan lang
(many tongues)   Icould'vesaidit   (sorry)
alph ph phabets   ssssigns   let lett letters

(The poem reaches
   past Babel babble
      back to the Word
         and beyond to sounds
            spinning like planets
               and pulsating stars

The spirit is pure sound
   the rumble that chases
      tree-splitting lightning
         heard or not

Words for this run blocker
   between sensation and understanding
      a highway posted with signs
         the smuggler disobeys

The perfect poem has no words
   cannot be trapped, uttered, seen
      but sings in the sleep of the poet's
         prehistory)

Poetry in Tupperware

stuff a spaghetti tube
with anapaests and dactyls

fill a pastel beaker
with red metaphors

chill 'till clichéd

stanza stackers
orange peel rhymers
a lifetime guarantee
not to crack under pressure

open a nest of synthetic savers
listen for bits of dreams
birds chirping in their eggs
sea surging in a conch
plants singing to the sun
sap rising to the tap

the hissing sound
of poetry escaping
in the afternoon

Dorothy Livesay and the Cyclops

The Great Canadian Poetry Weekend,
Collingwood, 07/06/80

Speed   One   Clap!

      Waiting to be   /   an independent woman

She waves the book, vortex of her vision,
poetry her weapon against bandaged microphones
her frail old crone's voice halted in mid-leap
across a sea of quartz lamps
by a prancing two-headed freak
his skull locked through the eye
to a gargantuan black-looped brain
a futuristic cyclops cradled in hands
of the automaton, who scales the rafters
in service to the godhead lens

She swallows, clears her throat
The CBC will take her
into the rec rooms of Canada
a celebrity before she dies

      He sent me home   /   to do dishes

On stage behind her the cyclops
aims past the glistening penumbra of her hair
into the audience extras who fancy themselves
going coast to coast
and look appropriately intense

and to mark its directorial debut
this whirring apex of evolution
slightly separates from the almosthuman
who upstages her by adjusting his glasses
with a vertical push of his middle finger
(the mediaman is the message)

then slaps together the tripod legs
in front of the sign which says
PLEASE! Poetry is being read

A tape runs on, lights blaze
and the disenchanted cannot hear

     The woman   /   I am

the thin plaint of imagination
that rendered her world alive
before modernity processed it to
segments between commercials

Literary Limits

Mr J sat reading by the window in his tower
when he noticed seven storeys down
near the edge where the grass slopes
off the yellow-leafed escarpment
a young man in blue blazer and beige pants
and a young woman in brown jacket and blue jeans
lying together
kissing;
not the kind you find on page 90
but kisses that were whole conversations
in the high afternoon haze.

Stephen Dedalus spoke from the book:
"A day of dappled seaborne clouds ...
The phrase and the day and the scene
harmonized in a chord."

Mr J would not agree
until the lovers had gone.

7th floor, Brock University Library

Poetry Reading

remembering Milton Acorn

He opens his bag
like Bethune in a lecture hall
glassy eyed, sweating,
plunging into cadavers
slashing his own skin
a wounded warrior
returned to the front
painting his martyrdom
with the taste of blood.
Someday they'll sculpt his monument
and chisel only the sculptor's name.

The World Is Always Being Born

A goldfish discovers her world for the first time
with every turn around the bowl
her brain is so small.

When bill bissett mentioned salmon farming
no not salmon farming – salmon, farming –
I thought I saw her start.
But then she swam past
and that notion was gone.

And when Shane Rhodes told of a Mexican father
naming his son Usmail (as in Call me Oosmail)
from a cancellation mark on a stamped letter
the goldfish opened her mouth.
But at once her laugh was swamped
and she swam past again.

And when bill chanted and rattled his rattle
the fish bobbed in fish time
as though he were speaking her language.
But then she felt the impulse to move on.

Every pass is new
every moment without context
the same old never the same old.
She must be in an ecstasy of wonder
her eyes wide open
her tiny brain always on.

Every poem is a new day
its discovery among the details
a moment of astonishing clarity.
Surprise is the daily bread
of poets and goldfish.

Beyond the Pride

You may allow me moments, not monuments.
—John Newlove

3000 miles from Nelson
somewhere between *The Pride* and
"Harry just can't that's all"
he throws back a double vodka
and tells of a cab fare that cost him
168 dollars, all of his reading fee but two,
and how he talked the driver into taking a cheque
and never wrote in the tip.

Like harmonica blues
blown by an accountant
he tells of his tie returned from Pat Lane.
He'd tied it round a bicycle two years back
at Pat's place, and now he can't remember
if he was locking up the bike
or the crossbar was his neck.

Past times with the dollar boys
he mainstreets with old poems.
Uncertain where he's touched down
he talks of Halifax in Hamilton
the Mears Island massacre
BC politics of any stripe
no difference, no point.

Somewhere beyond the pride he flies
over the shield's granite, the prairie's sweep

chasing horizons home
to the mountains at his back;
home from this costume party
coloured in forest wheat and rock
whose guests drift through like headlines.

Sleep heavy, proud poet
the score is with you or against you
tomorrow is just another city
and what is left
you still can love.

26/04/85

I Am Not Your Man

Leonard Cohen interviewed by Jian Gomeshi 16/04/2009

Before I was old, you didn't ask me
how I felt about dying.

Now, being both old and a poet,
I ought to know.

I answer with words you don't use –
the alliterative "can't command the consequences"

I want the truth to sound like me.
We are all caught in this charade of slogans.

I can't abide glory, but glory pays the bills.
Trophy, atrophy. Rest is how the rust gets in.

I wear the cap on Goy TV.
Were you expecting striped pyjamas?

Beyond the horizon everything comes together
into nothing but survival. Hallelujah.

If you fall prey to pretty virgin words
you can lie, really lie.

The teller and the tale.
Shape-shifting. Myth making.

"Get anything interesting?" I ask.
The crew want lunch.

Counting Down to Zero

For Robert Zend

… but then, at my feet, the sun
drowns in a rock pool:
swamped by the night tide
and almost expired
it looks to me to release it
with a slight turn of my glance
to save the world from freezing in darkness
so great is my power

… but just then, someone
passes a fluff of cloud
over my head and under the sun
so that to free the sun
I should have to fly
twenty miles due east very fast
and carry the rock pool with me

… but then, and what's more, someone
sends a cold chill down my spine
to warn me my moments here on this rock –
the rock by the pool where the sun
is dying I know, though I cannot see it
for the cloud above my head –
my moments are numbered
some flight director is counting
down to zero
and my disappearance

… but then, sometime during the count
though I cannot hear exactly when
a malfunction, I suppose
disperses the chill and the cloud
and again I see the sun
still in the pool
hoping to be saved
by a slight turn of my glance

… but then I could be wrong:
the fact is it's summer
there are hundreds of pools
in each one a sun
in a lemon lycra bathing suit
lying on an air mattress
sipping a martini
and watching the clouds
on their morning break.
Not one of them would jump
if I turned my head and yelled
"OK, everyone out of the pool."

For Earle Birney

At his typewriter on the roof
of his house in the bush
in the heat

        naked

but for a straw hat
he stops

        again

looks down the long lake –
a tourist boat in close
binoculars at the rail.

When there is no escape
and the examiners come

        he writes

tip your hat.

This Poem

for Joe Rosenblatt, Pat Lane, Milton Acorn, Earle Birney,
P.K. Page, Leonard Cohen, Irving Layton, Dorothy Livesay,
Gwendolyn MacEwen, Eli Mandel, David McFadden, bp
Nichol, John Newlove, Alden Nowlan, Al Purdy, Ray Souster,
Robert Zend, Miriam Waddington, Robert Kroetsch, and
Matt Cohen and Austin Clarke and John Herbert and the rest

This poem is not about silence
or the exegesis of silence.
It is not a critique of silence
or an appropriation of silence.
It is not silence redux.
It is neither the question nor the answer.
the omega nor the alpha of silence.
It is not the philosophy or psychology of silence.
It is not the silence of libraries and cemeteries
or the silence of tomorrow's eclipse.
It is not the effect of silence in space
or the pump of silence in the blood.
It is not the vow of a celibate novice,
or the 'e' at the bottom of the Alphabits box.

This poem

        is

                silent

Part 6
keening calls

ever and over

cling to the rim of the ding dong bell
ever and over revolving together
sun-blistered moon-hard heaven and hell
lover and liver and devil-giver

no rescuer now, no use to begrudge
while others stand mute in the shepherd's fold
the stable and hearth, where home is a ledge
the dividing line between straw and gold

high on the mountain of ice and fire
and midnight horizons to stumble over
ever and over, over together
it's over for ever, for over it's ever

time is a chance they might not choose
space depends on their point of view
on the go-around, up-down, ding-dong bell
the beckoning, deafening, dong-ding bell

bell   bell   bell   bell

The Death of Marriages

The marriages sprawl along the beach
sand sliding from their monstrous flanks
their eyes crusted in surf

marriages that couldn't walk out of the sea
nor roll back to the close deeps
and keening calls of brothers and sisters.

Small gatherings of people watch
the great waste. Children
climb ropes up to their backs
and pry at blow holes trying to see inside.
Some plot to return and thieve
a souvenir tooth. Some
listen, afraid
they are still alive.

A girl strokes her chocolaty hand
behind an eye and sings
a lullaby to the sleeping thing;
by morning only she remains
staring at the emptied sea.

A Bitch of a Marriage

She's quiet now, this old bitch of a marriage
the heart rapid in her soft hairs
the leathered eyes fogged.
You can see she's starving
though there's food in her bowl.

Yet sometimes her ears perk
like the pup chasing its tail
the sleek body darting and dropping
so fast you backtrack to catch her
the paws spread to spring off again.

When you come in, she no longer hears you.
Asleep, she warms the house from her rug.
Her feet flick to runaway dreams.
These days you wave the door in her face
before she'll climb the treacherous steps.

She came with the house
before there were children
and hardly a bed.
You love the old bitch
you rub your face
against her head.

One morning you'll wake to see that she's died.
You hope to discover her body still warm.
To lift the cold carcass would break you.

Grey March

A dappled cat
disgusted with chirping and rain
gazes inside at the Tiffany lamp
the woman, and four limp tulips
that yesterday trumpeted
the passing of a marriage.

The cat wails. The metal eyes
gleam, then drift
as it hunches down
against the damp pane.

Movers

He, showing his strength, struggles on the end
of my filing cabinet, lead heavy though empty, his
shoulders creased by the sharp edge

orders me to grasp the other end from underneath
and tilt it toward him, he knows how to lift
steel, he worked the summer in a fabricating plant
night shift mostly, cycling at 3:30 a.m. through
fog or rain or pitch of new moon, heedless at
fifteen and saving for a motorcycle, saving to
pay me back

and as I heave the metal block to tolerable height
he backs me up, across the lawn to the steps;
we jerk the thing upright into this strange place
littered with debris from twenty years of husbanding.

A liquid bead rolls off his chin
pings the metal and courses
down the cabinet side toward me
shrinking and stuttering
until past halfway it stops
weak and staring
then disappears the moment
we manhandle the brute into position.

Trying the drawer latch I say
In a couple of years I'll be helping you.
The drawer stays shut.
One of us has pressed in the lock
and I curse the stupid thing
that has connected us.

The Letter

all things come of thee, and of thine own have we given thee
—1 Chronicles 29:14

Today my son handed me a letter
written 40 years past to my then wife –
he'd come across it going through her stuff –
about the trouble we made for ourselves
when we were young, free, and wanted more.

A latecomer to our fractured marriage
he would not have known our history
of lies, deceit, pretence, apologies.
It named those we had loved and lost, and now
he understands what presaged our divorce.

Awkward to have your boy, become a man,
suddenly discover all your old sins
when you've spent your life hiding them.
I give it back. He tells me he'll shred it.
He doesn't admit he ever read it.

Yet life requires both light and dark: some say
a good Jew thanks God for the Holocaust.
Confession, forgiveness, absolution –
mere stepping stones to opportunity
to show my son no more am I that man.

Leaving Athens

39 hours through
the sun's white paralysis
the starless night;
the train offers no escape.
The valley's tunnel shrinks like a mine shaft
the air thins, my throat closes
blood throbs faster in my neck
my breath lurches in short gasps
a silent sudden suffocation.
Unstoppable as a mountain cataract
my tears course down her face in the glass.

The train carries me deeper
a captive cashiered from the Plaka's hustle
Syntagma's grey cafes
Sounion's sunset melancholy
screaming to return to her.
The drone of engines
the clacking rails
inexorable as the black peaks
that spear a cold quarter moon
drifting along beside me.

Shepherd fires flare
like tiny matches
struck on a dark cloak.
Border guards take my passport.
I find no solace
from this choking obsession
and the cruel stare of the one
I have shamed by my betrayal.

The corridor is crammed
with stinking bodies.
I clamber over them
to the end of the car
through the door
to a platform
I can step off
into the secretive hills.

She is no illusion. In pink robe
out on the stoop to wave goodbye
to launch me on this madness
that can have no destination
unless the train reverses itself
like iron drawn to a lodestone,
to Athens, and to her.

Holding On

Taking apart my MG bolt by bolt
is a winter preoccupation.
Ripping out carpet glued down since 1970
the year I fell in love with Athens
and a girl who looked like Joan Baez
and wept upon leaving them behind.

The carpet seems welded to the metal
unwilling to break its 37-year bond
with the floor. It pulls up handfuls
of rust dust, and just by luck
leaves no holes behind.

She e-mailed me today
wants to get together soon
before the car is fully restored.
They say when you fall so hard
you do not know the one you love.

She has denied all these years
any resemblance to Joan
until now. A picture I sent her
reminds her of her youth
when she brushed her long hair back
and nursed her first born
in the Greek summer heat.
I put the picture in my album
after the MG insurance photos.

Canada is wrong for an MG:
no winding roads lined with hedgerows
too few top-down days
and the killer winter salt.
I may not know where the bolts go
how to put Humpty back together
or what if anything the new interior
will change in the ride.

But when I'm alone and driving
along escarpment concessions
careful not to lose the muffler
in the occasional potholes
and my hair tangles and stings my eyes
and the sun burns white hot on the door rail
sometimes, sitting beside me, there's Joan
singing *The green green grass of home.*

Reading Glasses

Looking up from the page I see
you in every blur of passers-by
a purple puff of silk around your neck
your slender legs, grace in every step.

Under grey saints that harbour the homeless
rubbies self-medicate from paper bag bottles.
Anyone can be anyone in this city.
I am stateless, persona non grata
among people checking messages
reading on a bench, stopping in for coffee
chatting with one who assembles sandwiches.

And there you are, crossing the street
carrying a bag this time, a purse next.
Will you not once come sit with me,
watch the evening light becalm the street?
We could talk about a movie one of us has seen
between us the faint scent of sandalwood.
I wouldn't mind if you checked your watch.
Under the table our knees might touch.

We were never here –
an Antonioni ending
of cash registers and car horns –
I take off my reading glasses.
You walk past. I see you.

Return of the Perseids

The ways we miss our lives are life.
—Randall Jarrell

One August night
we caught sky streakers
in our hands like fireflies
and released them
back to the stuck stars.

Winter's last sundown
I run to your window –
the candles out
your face nestled in feathers.

I scuff my feet
on the gravel shoulder
and search out of season
for those star children
that blazed a path to greet us.

Part 7

beneath the civil skin

The Aristocrat and the Prodigal Son

For my father

In twilight's silence at the edge of thought
in a mansion of many metaphors
Belief stirs awake.

Leaves float down like gathering birds.
The clock turns back to reclaim the present
invitation to the world to reconsider.

Doubt returns home through the servants' entrance
while the gardener at the gate
shines his lantern on passers-by.

In the evening, both debate
who will win the oncoming night.
Each begs the other to listen.
Belief invokes the probable impossibility
of life in a crucible;
Doubt suspects Belief cheats at games of chance.

Belief tells the old stories in the dancing firelight
when people spoke with all living things,
stories about who shall tend the garden
and what cataclysm will end the world.

Unfortunate Doubt makes up new punch-lines,
pokes holes in the red coals with his staff
and drinks wine from his half-empty flask.

Tomorrow is uncharted territory,
a mirrored self-portrait, the halves of the face
a reversed labyrinth with no way out.

Sometimes the morning finds them
asleep in each other's arms.
Sometimes the morning doesn't come at all.

Dementia

My father was a civilized man.

A man who but for his father's call
had been a minister not a gardener,
who but for his government's expropriation
had been a nurseryman, not a salesman.

The man who drove me in tears to my singing lesson
knowing that my despair at not being able
to reach the high C or hold the two minute breath
would be erased by my teacher's not minding,
and that secretly I would wear my practised talent
as a badge of courage when peers shunned me.

A man who defended to bishops priests and deacons
the King James Bible and the Book of Common Prayer
who appealed to the Queen for intervention
when a premier held his province to ransom;
a man who stood for something.

What then to make of his *jew-boy* or *coloured*,
the racist attack against the hospital visitor,
the pit of snakes writhing below his paralysed feet
the bombs and burning buildings
in the war still raging in his head?
Had his sanity not sentenced
these barbarisms to the darkness
where evil is stored
beneath the civil skin?

Then civilization is a delusion to clothe us,
the chasm between *is* and *ought*
as easily filled by evil as by good:
the evil that seems harder to forget,
the good less than eager to forgive.

A civilized man was my father.
I loved him too late
and told him so to ease his passing.

Driving into a Cemetery on Father's Day

The lanes may merge or diverge at any moment.
You think you're driving to the West End pub
when you're channelled right, down the bay road.
You turn into the bone yard to correct your mistake
and are led through a puzzle of one way paths
a labyrinth of stones, monuments, statuary
of the city's royalty on the high ground
over Cootes Paradise, as though they deserve
to command a view of their piece of heaven.

It's a vantage my father would have liked
had he been whole and alive above ground
not a pile of dust and bits of bone
leftovers from the dissecting table, stored
in a common vault, named not for his gift
but for the institution that accepted his body.

This is   my body   given   for you
he said every Sunday, and now it was true.

Out beyond the rivers of red and yellow lights
fish splash after flies, a heron stands watch,
unseen creatures wake, night choruses rise,
the evening sinks toward darkness,
and mortal thoughts are put to sleep.

Breathe

      in the morning sun   a light beam
falls on your face   then you see
      what you are taking   into your lungs
asterisks & ampersands   commas & curlicues
      dots & dashes   air swirling with specks
like clouds of mating midges   when you thought
      you were breathing oxygen

the bad with the good   out of sight out of mind
      motes riding your blood   looking for a roost
a way off the coaster   into something permanent
      something inevitable   something successful
              cancer

      nothing is pure   everything's contested
the end comes   not in a shaft of light
      but a fire-curtain   in slow descent
since Act One   when expectations exited
      after the reveal   the audience leaves
the show closes   on a one night stand
      new dust spackles   blue lips
           in the morning sun

Things I Do to Miss You

park on my side of the driveway
sleep on my side of the bed
say "we" and "our house"
leave your voice on the answering machine
shop for more Pearl Bailey (pearl barley)
dry myself with your bath towel
turn down the TV so as not to wake you
leave your office door shut not to disturb you
go in anyway to disturb you
check my coins for your collectable quarters
wear your Haida key chain as a medallion
wear your two-rings charm on a gold chain
do your 1000 piece Christmas jigsaw
play your corny Christmas classics once
hang your stocking from the mantel
with mine and the cat's
try to donate a kidney to your brother
because you would have but could not
fill the feeder to attract a cardinal
thank you when one comes

Painting Over Smoke

BROWN

The stains have been curing for
eighteen years
age spots
seared into plaster.

Lighter rectangles mark
outlines of accolades
a diploma, a certificate
in this emptied tomb.

Rivers of tar dripped down walls
while you studied blood cells
phoned the all-night OHIP lady
rescued Zelda more than once
and stopped a bereaved neighbour
from his planned demise
through the window at 3 a.m.

– he had botched
a 30 pill attempt
to end his life
join his wife
and was upping the ante
to 100 for next time –

the brown gunk thickening
at the corners
along the seams

inside the lungs
black as a miner's.

Chemical over chemical
I scrub away your murderer.
Ammonia and vinegar
turn cloudy in minutes.
I swallow the fumes
breath by acrid breath.

WHITE

The walls and ceiling
primed a wide-angle white
to hide your addiction.
They make me small,
who could not turn it around
while there was time.

The grime obliterated
beneath the glare
all trace of you erased
everywhere space
white on white on white
a perfect purposeless purgatory.

GREEN

The painter rolls on your favourite colour;
he could paint paradise in a mine shaft.
Green makes food out of light.

New, clean, my spare room
ready for someone to come
an overnight guest
ready for you.

You can stay here
free at last
from the hundred cancers
from the browning of Everything.

You can be calm here.
You can breathe involuntarily.
You will not die here.

I'll leave the door open.

October 2017

Burning Chair

Under the spreading locust limbs, a chair
old, rustic, of bent vines and cedar boards
host to rampant English ivy entwined
around its feet, winding through its spines
sucking marrow from its bones

the splits and nicks and splintered shards
the frame twisted as if by hurricane
seat planks broken from their moorings
fallen askew, showing rot in their ends.

In the cool autumnal breeze
leaves drift onto the wreck
like pear-shaped daubs of yellow
paint, a last gasp of quiet joy.

The pieces look easy to pry apart
break into fire grate lengths
but brads and spikes rust firm in old wood
and ivy grips tight. This will take
a pry bar, a sledge, and still
the boards split only with the grain
the vines will not snap across my knee.
The chop saw sparks against a nail
a defiant complaint of rubble denied
the chance to follow its own timely decline.

Flames cast out sweet cedar's scent
the same as perfumes your hope chest
full of fine fabrics for a hopeless future.

Ashes, like your own remains
handed to me in a cardboard box
with a ziplock bag half full of white dust
your pulverized and powdered bones.

Once again I must turn the earth, find a place
below the surface, suited to receiving salvage.

October 2016

Communion

I come across a Mission in a southern state
near a nation whose gold was stolen
and faith imposed by ball and blade.
The Spanish chapel looks like the Alamo
before it was shot apart by the Mexican army.

White-faced adobe walls house empty pews
red paint worn through by the soles of the pious
a garlanded Virgin mother and child
food on the table of the last supper
cherubs wielding wands or playing banjos.

Beneath a saint or a risen christ
among the rows of votive candles
a single flame burns cranberry vigil
a woman prays in the sacred light.

I choose to rest in the solace
of feast, mother, and penitent
and commune with my beloved
thankful she travels with me
to any foreign sanctuary.

A Troubadour's Exit Strategy

200 years to find a plan
— Stephen Hawking

A wild last waltz
to reach the stars
4.2 light years away
where there are no pink candy Christmas trees
no Rocky Horror Picture Show
no marigolds and daisies

All the world's a stage
and we're leaving on the next one[*]
Baby pack light[**]
a caravan of emigrants
no tear gas no fences
the planet gets a reprieve

celebrate the lottery winners
the cobbled together astronauts
the at-all-costs survivors
who made it on board
award them medals so their children
learn life belongs to the chosen

---

[*] Perth County Conspiracy, 1972, *The Perth County Conspiracy Alive*, "Stratford People"
[**] Jon Brooks, 2018, *No One Travels Alone*, "Proxima B"

the abandoned will be anonymous
the missing yesterday's fishwrapper
the murdered victims of circumstance
Will despots go home to spend time with family?
Will autodidacts hunker down in caves?

What would you bring?
I'd bring you but
you're already there
streaming the universe
from cellular to numinous
we are all gone to spirit

A Tinge of Blue

Stage Four

On the ---- day of your confinement
"I don't want to live like this."

I heard you
and signed the paper

> There you are in the batter's box
> glaring at the pitcher
> hands not giving an inch of choke
> leaning into it, ready to lunge –
>
> last inning at bat
> he rifled a line drive
> at your solar plexus
> Slo-pitch! Rec League! Mixed!
>
> Now it's his fear you taste

On the ---- day of your confinement
"I don't want to die."

I heard you
I said "I don't want you to die."

> From the bleachers I laughed
> when you came up to bat
> their infield shifting right
> they never guessed wrong

or you slid into base
ignoring the raspberry
like it never happened

or you forced the out at home
and threw a laser to second
for the third out, triple play
the day you made the papers

37 trophies and 5 plaques
and still your dad did not watch
you play the man's game

On the morning you died
I wasn't there

When I came
you were gone

I did not kiss your forehead
or maybe I did
my eyes could not ask
for your lips
already turned

Stage Door

April 23rd, three years later

Sunrise, a blood sweep
sliced by the fiery fingernail
quickly pales to mauves and oranges
as the disc swells
painting the underside of clouds
over and over
in its urgency.

Last year's leaves flit about on a gust of breeze
like impatient sparrows frantic
for food, a mate, a home
in the sun's warm promise.

Two mourning doves already partnered
walk a thick branch. In a flurry of wings
he settles on her, then sated, turns away.

Daffodils bow their heads to the polished grass.
Under the stalks of the pink David Austin
time has done its work:
no trace of your ashes remains.

The cardinal rocks the feeder
flies off to fetch his wife.
Someone has whitewashed the sky.

Part 8
*Intihuatana**

... and the yonge sonne
Hath in the Ram his half cours y-ronne
Than longen folk to goon on pilgrymages
— Geoffrey Chaucer, 1380, Prologue to *The Canterbury Tales*

---

* a granite prism pointed directly at the sun, a kind of astronomic observatory used to divine calendar divisions and agricultural seasons. In the Quechua language: *inti* means "sun," and *wata-* is the verb root "to tie, hitch (up)." Hence inti watana is literally an instrument to "tie up the sun." At midday on the equinoxes March 21st and September 21st, the sun stands above the pillar, casting no shadow. All the Inkan intihuatanas were destroyed or damaged by Pizarro's conquistadors, except the one at Machu Picchu.

Prologue

Myth is written on the spine of the Americas.
Long ago, in the time of making
the Word was unspoken.
The Word was nothing
and the something that came from that.
The Word was the foetal murk
and the emergent cry into light.
The People lived in darkness and were afraid.
Viracocha, lord of all, in gleaming garments
said "Let there be day, let there be night!
Let there be dawn, let it grow light!" *
Condor, oldest of all flying creatures
brought them the sun on his back
but the blazing fireball singed his feathers
and he dropped it in flight.

The People found it deep in the mountains
and tried to blow the fire out
but they fanned the flames brighter
and blew the ball up into the sky, raining gold.
When the sun sensed greed approaching
it whistled and cried out.
Then Condor plucked out the eyes
of the thieves with his beak
and spat them into the night sky
never to see the gold they came for.

---

* Translated from one of the Sacred Hymns of Pachacouti, 1438-1471,
 Inkan ruler, son of the Sun. During his reign, the Inka expanded from
 mud hut villages to the largest empire in the Americas.

He stripped their backs with his talons
and left their bodies to bake in the sun.
From their teeth he made a rattle
from their bones flutes, and from their skin a drum.
Then the People danced before the powerful Condor.
But the sun, looking down, could see his loneliness.

Imagine a tree, living in beauty
felled by storm, its first death.
Cut into fire logs to warm a family
it becomes ash to nourish soil and seeds.
These two visible deaths we count.
Others may reach past our lifetimes
past our planet's end, where existence
and assuming it are one and the same
where there's nothing in heaven and earth
but saying makes it so. Word spoken.

this magnificent   remnant
    an ordered   wreckage   the bedrock
      implicates   a beyond   upon
        cultivates   a mystery   itself
                insists

Edifices of belief will be built to explain
what was once declared into being.
But ruins are ruins, an alpine haven
a few hundred years before
the jungle swallows it whole.
They say "Attention, witness!
You thought you were right.
You are an ant tunnelling in that tree.

You don't know how you got here, where you are
when you are not, or where you will be."

In their beginning, men roped monoliths
dragged them up slopes
and offered their gods the blood of children.

Now, the quarry lacks cutters.
The royal tombs are robbed, the mummies stolen.
The dead lie with the snake or fly with the condor.

Caucasians wander the streets of Machu Picchu,
puff up and down steep flights of steps.
Backpackers pause between breaths
shoot selfies through windows to distant peaks
peer into burial chambers where old Quechua words lie
cup their hands in a fountain's 500-year trickle,
touch their forehead on the intihuatana
expecting a vision of the spirit world,
their savvy guide's promise.

Seen from deep in the canyon floor
the alabaster sun tracks a pale path.
Seen from high on the roof of the Andes,
the scarlet disk awakes from daybreak's fire
rolls through the blood sky to its white hot zenith
then sinks into sanguinary sleep
and the cold night of souls.

And so we climb pathways to our brightest star
and look back on our planet's blistered skin,
and consider whether that is all
we know and all we need to know.

Inka Trail

Nine hours a day we gasp rarefied air
coca leaves wadded like baccy in our cheeks
too far to turn back, no helicopter rescue
no escape, no priest's last rites.

Every hour, ghost runners in rainbow colours
lap us, their sandaled feet Andean cat quiet.
We press against the cliff side to let them pass.
"Hola" to the tourist who eyes every cobble
"Hola" to their backs, bent double
under cloth sacks woven by women
on backstrap looms to sling our supplies.

Inka roads thread the Andes from Ecuador to Bolivia
like khipu strings* knotted with secrets of empire
that Spanish rosaries could never untangle.
Walking the old routes, on worn stones
polished by feet of another's forbears
is like stepping in footprints the sea has raised
from the hard mud soup of another millennium
to see if they fit us, imagining
history in the closing mist
where there are no edges or borders
and we are all short-sighted ghosts.

---

* khipu: a string with knots tied in it, believed to record numbers, accounts, thoughts, and possibly stories and memories. The Inka did not have writing, and there is no corresponding Rosetta Stone to help us decode the khipus.

Porters descended from peasants or warriors;
a crime to be idle, a weakness to rest.
Did their ancestors in their brazen rightness
believe they could do anything –
build a city on a mountain crest –

                              would stop?
                    the sun
    so long as

All the young pilgrims long out of sight
air pumping their lungs, their skin soft, white;
I lift my boot high to clear the next ledge –
with methodical mechanical right foot left foot
I traverse three high passes in three days,
victory or defeat in every footfall.

Each evening my fellows applaud the arrival
of the scatterling, late to their table.
I've been eight hours staring at the ground.
My neck atrophied, I cannot look them in the eye.
At supper my left hand props up my head
so my right can spoon food to mouth. They ask
what this old man may put at risk next day.

Dead Woman's Pass

On the second day, for seven miles
of incremental ascent to 14,000 feet
I feel the sucking pull of stairs
the doubling weight of my hiker's boots
thin air and thinner desire.

Look to the firmament's welkin blue
lose your footing, fall into the abyss
a vertiginous drop to the ribboning river
its torrent silenced by mountainous heights.
Look to sure ground, every laddered inch
of this rough and tumble roller coaster
tests your limits, body and will.
When you're climbing, the road meanders
a slight suggestion of a way forward.
It's the road you're on, it puts you in your place.
You must have faith in where it leads.

Some hundred yards below Dead Woman's Pass
a trekker pulls up to catch her breath.
She has come to an impasse, a crisis of decision.
Fatigue cripples us both; we can't bridge the gap
between body's collapse and over-reaching vision.
We embrace as one figure, young girl, old man
two days from the citadel, drained of strength
huddled and hopeless, stranded in a high desert.
I lean into her, she weeps, our hearts keep
a staccato backbeat to the panic of despair.

At rest, I dream an ancestral courier
is running the cordillera of the Milky Way
carrying dispatches of conquest and betrayal.
I look to the night's open canopy.
A satellite passes, a pinprick of starlight
pushes apart the Southern Cross.
We are there too, bouncing messages
in the spaceland among sky fires.
We say 'We are.'

4 a.m. We break camp in the moonless pitch
our goal to reach Sun Gate by daybreak
and, if we are spared mists and fog, see
the ruined city rise from terraced slopes
straddle the saw-toothed ridge between peaks
that cradled a king and his servants and labourers
for a brief hundred years when the old world fell
to empire and cross, bullet and blade.

At the edge of the camp the trail falls away;
I must trust my life to a torch in my teeth
I am a child again, afraid of cellar stairs.
A faint yellow glow from the last of our tents
underlights branches of a single conifer
tall and wan, fuller at the head
with arms reaching out, palms open, an huaca*
here to curse and warn, or bless and protect.
I opt for the latter; the fear vanishes.

---

* huaca: a minor spirit which could inhabit just about any remarkable phe-
nomenon, such as a cave, a waterfall, large boulder, or tree.

I set down an offering of coca leaves
whisper 'Thank you' to my pagan ally
and, white-knuckled grip on the trekking poles
start to descend the rock-mined path
the last to arrive at the checkpoint where
I receive my souvenir passport stamp
and wait with the rest for the sky to brighten.

Sun Gate (Intipunku)

The last four hours in minimal visibility
I have stumbled along, last to the Gate.
The others, far ahead, pose on a table rock;
the bragging rights shot may entice their friends
to come touch the pillar that tethers the sun.

Behind them the city spills over the saddle
like a blanket someone has tossed and shaken;
the houses and temples tumble down
pell-mell upon the terraced defences
against seismic shocks and washout rains.

A crescent fire warms the mountain cauldron
flames the snow-caps, burns through mist
sweeps down to set the bastion ablaze.
Grazing llamas look up, swallow their spit.
Intihuatana awaits its moment.

The Temple of Three Windows

I am unconcerned with the primacy of three;
snake puma condor, underworld middle earth stars.
The image I want is now, is *you*.
"Something in the foreground?" I say.
"How do you sweep a dirt floor?" you say,
posing yourself in the temple's middle trapezoid.
My lens explores the tilt of your sunhat,
your shades on the brim like Orphan Annie's eyes,
your dimpled smile as you think of the joke.
The shutter clicks, and too quickly it's done.
The temple's vista, a mountain triptych
returns me to the discord of now and then
and the Girl in the Stone Window, triumphant.

The Temple of the Sun (Torreon)

What astounded the Inka was the newborn god
awake from his manger in the alpine mists
splaying his gold through the temple window
onto the altar where blood was spilled
on the winter solstice, June 21st.
Sunbeams rooted in knotted memory
stream upon this timely rock
to signal the arrival of the dry season.

Pachacuti's condor stirs in his cavern
rises from dirt, skates circles on the updraft
rides thermals up sugarloaf Hwayna Picchu
soars above frosted peaks and smoking craters
glides across the city to sleep near the Royal crypt.
The locals say his wings gather clouds.

Intihuatana, Hitching Post of the Sun

The high priest's face and hands lift in salutation
his back bowed in submission, a gold plate held aloft.
As the sun cycles through its quotidian
he invokes the harbinger numen to halt
hitch itself to the granite tongue
and track no lower in the winter sky.

If the deity will grant his plea – guarantee
another year's sustenance after deluge and quake
inflame the growing months, safe from conquistadors –
then this man's reach may exceed his grasp
his supplication alter the course of a star
for the sake not of heaven, but sunstruck harvest.

If the sun will stop for them, peons will break boulders
haul them uphill without horse or wheel
build a king's retreat for a thousand people
and in the same century abandon it.

And if you and I return on equinox, the sun may

stop

tie up

rest

cast no shadow

face us

bless us

Aguas Calientes

El Bar by the train tracks serves ceviche and cuy –
raw fish and roast guinea-pig – and chicha by the litre.
On the table a perpetually flowering orchid.

A child counts table crumbs one by one
as though they were days the sun sweats gold beads
or nights the moon weeps silver tears
gold and silver Pizarro never found.
The infant watches his young mother
sweep the crumbs into her hand.
He pulls at her arm, reaches for them
it's all that matters to him now.

Humans always manufacture meaning.
We build temples to gods we believe will favour us.
We sanctify whatever land we occupy.
What might have been this monumental wreckage?

For King Pachacuti, a royal estate
for the mason, interlocking joinery
for the farmer, irrigated pastures
for animals and captives, fate
for the virgins, service.
Rock haulers and stone cutters cannot foresee
the temple they are building. How can I
seeking respite from the crust of modern life
the smallness of oughts and soughts
know the mystery or what it means?

Stone, like the planet, erodes to dust;
tremors crack and crumble buildings
floods wash away bridges and people
human intentions are reinterred.
Pachamama, mother of the Earth
buries the legacy of a conquering empire.

I have made my pilgrimage to the fields of the sun.
A foreign visitor to be held in restraint
like Inti*, over the natural world
I have ascended this realm of towers and spires
and felt the sun bronze my skin.

Drops of sweat splash on the stones
at my feet. They darken with the stain.
My moment is in some way theirs.
I am defined by what my imagination eats.

---

* Inti: the Sun.

Notes

p. 83   "This Poem"
Joe Rosenblatt died on March 11, 2019. He was my
first mentor.

p. 108   "Painting Over Smoke"
Eighteen months after my wife died, I rid her office of
every trace of twenty-seven years of smoking, along
with her clothes, files, games, trophies, photos, books,
computers, and remembrances of things past.

p. 119   "Intihuatana"
In 2008 at the age of 64, and with assistance from guide
Ozzi Porcel and his crew, I hiked the four-day Inka Trail
to Machu Picchu.

Acknowledgements

The author acknowledges with deep gratitude the invaluable editorial guidance, observations, and insights of his talented literary friends, Chris Pannell, Gary Barwin, Don Mackenzie, Catherine Hunter, James Deahl, and his publisher, Michael Mirolla.

Some of these poems have appeared previously in books (*Reclamation* by David Haskins [Borealis Press, 1980], *This House Is Condemned* by David Haskins [Wolsak & Wynn, 2013], *Tamaracks: Canadian Poetry for the 21st Century* edited by James Deahl [Lummox Press, 2018]); multiple issues of several literary journals and magazines *(Canadian Author and Bookman, Canadian Forum, Carousel, Dream Catcher, Great Lakes Review, Hammered Out, How Exhilarating and How Close, Intrinsic, Lummox, More of Our Canada, Origins, Poetry Canada, The Saving Banister, Tower Poetry, Wee Giant, Windsor Review)*; and web sites (www.ditchpoetry.com, www.leafpress.ca, www.stephengill.ca/gazette.htm, www.stellarshowcasejournal.com, https://andreasgripp.wixsite.com/synaeresis, www.rootsmusic.ca, http://wolsakandwynn.ca/blog)

Awards

A shorter version of the *Intihuatana* suite of poems won the GritLIT Poetry Contest in 2015.

Intihuatana was shortlisted for the Vallum Chapbook Award 2016

"Morning Coffee At Station One" and "Driving into a Cemetery on Father's Day" received Honourable Mentions in the CAA Niagara Poetry Contest in 2016

My memoir *This House Is Condemned* (Wolsak & Wynn, 2013) was shortlisted for both the Non-fiction Award and the Kerry Schooley Award by Arts Hamilton in 2015

"I Am Not Your Man" won the Leonard Cohen Poetry Contest at www.rootsmusic.ca in 2012

"Urban Fox" won the Arts Hamilton Literary Award for Individual Poem in 2011

"Reclamation" won, and "Waiting" received Honourable Mention, in the Ontario Poetry Society's "Second Time Around Contest" in 2007.

"How to Write a Canadian Poem" won the Canadian Authors Association, Niagara branch poetry contest in 2007.

About the Author: In His Own Words

When I was seven in 1952, my teacher gave me a copy of Kenneth Grahame's *The Wind in the Willows* as a reward for catching up on math homework during the summer holiday. Each night I went to sleep with a chapter's worth of those class-conscious tweedy animals in my head. That same summer I read every adventure of Enid Blyton's mystery solving children, the Secret Seven and the Famous Five. When I sent her a question by mail, she posted back her reply in blue-black ink from a fountain pen on a postcard bordered with frogs and dragonflies and signed with her unique signature. Enid Blyton wrote to me! I knew I wanted to write too.

The next year, my family emigrated from England to Canada, to small town Beamsville, Ontario. I left behind eleven pets, from tortoises to a horse, and was permitted to bring one portable hamster, Monty (named after Field Marshall Bernard Law Montgomery), who sailed on a rabbit's boarding pass. I wrote an account of the sea voyage, which my new teacher brought round to the house to show my parents.

My affection for animals led me to imagine a working life as a veterinarian. It took only one trip to the vet college open house for its stinking formaldehyde, its brown bottles of pale organs, and its blood and guts operating rooms to cure me of that notion. So, of course, I became an English teacher, a career I loved for its uniting of literature and young minds, but one which necessarily put my writing on the back burner. The odd poem or story or review or educational text would sneak out into the published world, the odd contest would award me a prize, and I felt encouraged enough to continue. My first novel, still in the drawer, was a "young adult" adventure fantasy that in some metaphorical world paralleled my own growing up.

I took a hiatus from teaching to hone my craft as a writer. In the halcyon late 1970's in Toronto it was possible to get instruction from Canada's A-list authors. My mentors were Joe Rosenblatt, Austin Clarke, Matt Cohen, P.K. Page, Carol Bolt, Steve McCaffery, Phil Marchand and others. Playwright John Herbert invited a small group of us apprentices into his tiny Yonge Street apartment from noon to midnight one Saturday a month for a year to swap stories, critique each other's work, and listen to him hold court. One winter I taught John's Creative Writing course for him while he returned to the theatre. A story I asked Austin Clarke to read won First Prize in the CBC literary competition in 1977. A poem I wrote for Joe Rosenblatt was published in *Canadian Forum*, and became the title poem of my first book, *Reclamation*, from Borealis Press in 1980. My shelf began to fill with journals and publications that had accepted my work.

Publisher Noelle Allen at Wolsak and Wynn assembled some of the best pieces in *This House Is Condemned*, a literary memoir in stories, non-fiction, poetry, and a novella. The book was shortlisted for two Arts Hamilton Literary Awards in 2013.

A couple of years after that book's release my personal life fell apart. After protracted medical setbacks, my first wife and the mother of my two sons died in 2015. My second life partner since 1986 was diagnosed with stage four lung cancer. In March of 2016, emergency bypass surgery saved my life, but incapacitated me at the very time when my beloved needed me most. Six weeks later, at the age of 52 years, she died. I have written of the aftermath in the anthology *Locations of Grief: An Emotional Geography* (Wolsak and Wynn, 2020).

Blood Rises collects poems written during my life with her.

This book is made of paper from well-managed FSC® - certified forests, recycled materials, and other controlled sources.

 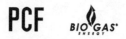